HART CRANE Poems selecte

Harold Hart Crane was born i
of his life in New York City, w
copy-writer. *White Buildings*, h   ......, appeared in
1926 and his most famous work, *The Bridge*, in 1930. A reaction
against the pessimism in T. S. Eliot's *The Waste Land,* it is a love
song to the myth of America and its optimism encapsulates the
excitement and energy of the Jazz Age. Hart Crane committed
suicide in 1932.

Maurice Riordan has published three collections of poetry – *A
Word from the Loki* (1995), *Floods* (2000) and *The Holy Land*
(2007) – and is co-editor of two anthologies, *A Quark for Mister
Mark: 101 Poems about Science* (2000) and *Wild Reckoning: an
anthology provoked by Rachel Carson's Silent Spring* (2004).

HART CRANE

Poems selected by
MAURICE RIORDAN

faber and faber

First published in 2008
by Faber and Faber Limited
3 Queen Square London WC1N 3AU

Typeset by RefineCatch Ltd, Bungay, Suffolk
Printed in England by CPI Bookmarque, Croydon

A CIP record for this book
is available from the British Library

ISBN 978–0–571–23803–3

10 9 8 7 6 5 4 3 2 1

Contents

LETTERS

Introduction

'Catullus *redivivus*, the Shelley of our age' – Robert Lowell

Hart Crane is the Romantic poet of the twentieth century. He shared a sense of cultural disjunction and historical crisis with Joyce and Eliot, the older contemporaries he most admired. He saw in the modern age a break with the values of the past, and he viewed with dismay the dominance in America of a materialist culture that betrayed its historic destiny. But his response was to commit himself to the transforming power of the imagination. He set out to write a great work that would re-establish the original ideal of America as the earthly Paradise. He believed, or at least he sometimes speculated, that consciousness itself could be transformed through the ecstatic medium of poetry. In his own memorable phrase, he belonged to 'the visionary company of love', to the lineage of Blake, Shelley and Keats – to which he added Whitman as his immediate American forebear. The role of the poet was heroic: to transcend human limitation; to inspire faith in the ideal; to achieve perfect eloquence. Crane's is a body of modern poetry that is shaped and determined, in its failures as well as its triumphs, by this singular and exalted sense of purpose.

The emergence of such a pure Romantic sensibility was not a predictable outcome when Harold Hart Crane first arrived in New York in 1916 from Cleveland, Ohio. Born in 1899, the only son of a sweet-manufacturer (his father is credited with inventing 'the mint with a hole') and a possessive beautiful mother, he had left home without graduating from high school, while his parents were in the process of a divorce. At his mother's prompting, he dropped the Harold in favour of Hart, her maiden name. His taste in poetry was *fin de siècle*: the title of his one published poem was 'C 33', a reference to the number of Wilde's prison-cell in Reading Gaol. He was an adventurous, troubled and somewhat neglected adolescent come to the big city to explore his sexuality as well as follow his declared calling as a poet.

This was the heyday of the 'little magazines', where a vigorous modern movement in American and international poetry was in full swing. The novice poet was exposed to its main practitioners and their precepts in the pages of *The Dial*, *The Little Review*, *Poetry* and numerous other imprints. Soon he was himself publishing accomplished restrained poems in the new manner, influenced by Eliot, and more so by Eliot's masters the Metaphysicals and the French Symbolists – a phase that reached a point of maturity with 'Praise for an Urn', written when he was still twenty-two.

Crane then reacted against what he saw as Eliot's pessimism, and its limitations, and set course towards a more 'positive . . . ecstatic goal'. In the next couple of years he began to form his own very distinctive style: in subjective lyrics, visionary in intent, that are so dense and associative it is difficult to paraphrase them and impossible to read them as narrative. Marianne Moore notoriously rewrote 'The Wine Menagerie' (not included here), before publishing it in *The Dial*. The puzzlement of his contemporaries led Crane to defend, and try to define, his new method:

> I may very possibly be more interested in the so-called illogical impingements of the connotations of words on the consciousness (and their combinations and interplay in metaphor on that basis) than I am interested in the preservation of their logically rigid significations at the cost of limiting my subject matter and perceptions involved in the poem.

This letter to the editor of *Poetry*, Harriet Monroe, shows him evolving what he termed the 'logic of metaphor'. Crane cites both Blake ('a sigh is a sword of an Angel King') and Eliot ('Every street lamp that I pass/ Beats like a fatalistic drum') as examples of how metaphor bypasses logic. But his own practice is closer to that of Mallarmé and Rimbaud in the sheer density of metaphor and also in its constant novelty of diction.

Crane then added another string to his rhetorical bow, a headlong syntactical impetus that he learned from the Elizabethan and Jacobean dramatists. The result is his best and most characteristic work, in the 'Voyages' sequence, in 'Repose of Rivers', and portions of *The Bridge*. 'Voyages II' remains his signature poem, a lyric unequalled in the language for its metaphorical richness and rhythmic drive:

Mark how her turning shoulders wind the hours,
And hasten while her penniless rich palms
Pass superscription of bent foam and wave, –
Hasten, while they are true, – sleep, death, desire,
Close round one instant in one floating flower.

Bind us in time, O Seasons clear, and awe.
O minstrel galleons of Carib fire,
Bequeath us to no earthly shore until
Is answered in the vortex of our grave
The seal's wide spindrift gaze toward paradise.

The overflow of association here stands up to scrutiny; and it is this fine coordination of words together with their overall movement, the sure musical stride of the lines, that make 'Voyages II' and a handful of Crane's other poems his enduring contribution to English verse.

'Voyages' celebrates, and elegises, a relatively happy love affair. By then he was already thinking about a long poem that 'roughly, concerns a mystical synthesis of "America"'. He struggled sporadically with this ambitious project, reading widely, reworking its visionary climax, but not making much headway with it. In the summer of 1926, he secluded himself on the Isle of Pines, a tiny tropical island (now called Isla de Juventud) offshore from Havana, where his maternal family had a house. Prospects for *The Bridge* didn't look good: 'The form of my poem rises out of a past that so overwhelms the present with its worth and vision', he wrote to his mentor Waldo Frank, 'that I'm at a loss to explain my delusion that there exist any real links between that past and a future destiny worthy of it.' But a month later he had changed his tune: 'Hail brother! I feel an absolute music in the air again, and some tremendous rondure floating somewhere.' The storm had broken: in a Duino-like surge of inspiration, he produced in six weeks more than half of *The Bridge*, as well as most of his remaining good individual poems.

Crane's is a poetry of heightened perception, of ecstasy, of language itself in a molten state of metaphor. He drank while he wrote, he played Ravel's *Bolero*, he stomped about shouting out and testing his lines. He got himself worked up. There is more than a hint of a deliberate *déreglement des sens* about his spells of strenuous composition, which could go on for days without let-up. More than on these props, however, he relied on the stimulus of emotional turmoil, on the swings of mood that were caused freely enough by both his parental relationships and his love affairs. And it was a specific intensity of stimulation that he needed – one that carried him over the threshold into the logic of metaphor, into what he considered a visionary state of inspiration. The goal is absolute eloquence, poems that offer 'a single, new *word*, never before spoken'. His lyric poems often rehearse this ascent to vision. They act out a personal myth in which the lover's suffering raises him to a state which is purifying, and death-like, an extinction of the self. Thus he is united with the Absolute and is rewarded with poetic vision, with 'the Word'.

The Bridge purports to give this notion of poetic ecstasy 'epic' implications. The poet takes on the hero's role and seeks to duplicate his experience for 'America'. The sequence of poems enacts a double quest. In its first half, the poet-narrator sets out to discover and explore the body of the continent, symbolised as Pocahontas. This phase reaches its climax when the narrator, now an Indian brave, is sacrificed and united in death with Pocahontas. It is a fertility myth: the moment of sacrifice is one of union with the earth goddess and leads to ecstatic vision. In this primitivist part of the poem, Crane's writing is sure and often beautiful, and it gathers up many strands of nature, history, legend and symbol into a wonderfully rich and elaborate synthesis – and that first span of *The Bridge*, up to and including 'Cutty Sark', is surely one of the triumphs of modernist poetry, comparable in its way to other characteristic works of the 1920s, such as Yeats's *The Tower* and MacDiarmid's *A Drunk Man Looks at the Thistle*. (Some indication of the latter's affinity is implied by the fact that MacDiarmid transcribed the concluding lines of 'Ave Maria' and published them as his own poem.)

The second half of *The Bridge* is another matter. Now the poet-narrator returns to New York City and to twentieth-century America. The quest is for a myth in the actual historical world that would parallel the sacrifice of the Indian and so redeem America and point to its visionary destiny. Crane described the longest section here, 'Cape Hatteras', as 'a sort of hymn to Whitman'. It addresses Whitman as the visionary-aviator. The climax enacts the death in battle of an airman (who is also the visionary poet). This, then, is the tragic sacrifice that revitalises Whitman's vision of America. Crane struggled with this part of the poem and his eventual writing of it is strained, often absurdly so. Other parts of this second movement are more successful, notably 'The Tunnel', but it is 'Cape Hatteras' that jeopardises the poem's ultimate optimism, because it cannot offer a convincing counterpart to the mythic past.

The Bridge is a failure. It can accurately be called a 'heroic' failure because of its Romantic aim. It is also remarkable, I think, for the intelligence that makes it just about plausible as a concept. I've selected from it on the basis of individual poems. I've omitted 'Cape Hatteras' among others – although I have included 'Atlantis', the culminating 'visionary' poem. Crane's rhetoric here is more forced than it is in the best passages. Even so, it makes a magnificent noise, and it belongs to that distinguished sub-genre of poems inspired by the Brooklyn Bridge.

I've also given space to poems that are somewhat marginal to Crane's main concern. He was a sympathetic observer and he had an ear for everyday speech, qualities which would have developed over a longer and less narrowly directed career and would have given his work a more common register. I've selected as well from Crane's letters, because I think he is one of the great letter-writers among poets. He carried on an intense literary correspondence, notably with his poet-friends Allen Tate and Yvor Winters, that often clarifies his aims or glosses particular poems. But he could also write helpfully about his work – reminding one of Keats – to his unliterary housekeeper on the Isle of Pines. This is the 'Aunt Sally Simpson' who appears in 'The River', and the last person to whom he wrote.

Crane visited London once, briefly, in the winter of 1929, when he had Christmas dinner with Laura Riding and with Robert Graves and his wife Nancy Nicholson on their houseboat in Hammersmith. Graves and Riding had included him in *A Survey of Modernist Poetry* (1927). But that has proved the high watermark so far of Crane's reception in Britain. F. R. Leavis found his 'symbolism amounts to nothing more than a turgidly rhetorical "shall" ' and judged *The Bridge* 'a wordy chaos, both locally and in sum'. When his *Complete Poems* was published in 1984, Douglas Dunn deplored 'his wilful wordage', and 'scant regard for syntax' and wondered if there had ever been 'a less thrifty poet'.

Critics of Crane have often used such terms of moral disapproval, on the assumption perhaps that excesses of style must have a parallel in private life. This is partly the case with Crane, though he had in fact a kind and generous nature and did little harm to anyone except himself. But that harm was considerable. By his mid-twenties he was alcoholic and promiscuous, prone to wild frightening tantrums and bouts of paranoia, too often the victim of beatings and robbery. He exasperated his friends – many of them married couples – with cycles of quarrelsomeness and contrition. His behaviour got worse as inspiration eluded him and he lost confidence in his work. He struggled to finish *The Bridge* and, once finished, he wrote little in the remaining two years of his life.

The last turbulent year was spent in Mexico, with the support of a Guggenheim fellowship. There he fell in love with Peggy Baird, an old friend and estranged wife of his friend Malcolm Cowley. He recovered briefly – true to the Romantic paradigm – his creative energy. The result was 'The Broken Tower', one of his finest and most poignant poems, with its intimation of a restorative love and poetic recuperation:

> Is it she
> Whose sweet mortality stirs latent power? –
>
> And through whose pulse I hear, counting the strokes
> My veins recall and add, revived and sure
> The angelus of wars my chest evokes:
> What I hold healed, original now, and pure . . .

It was not to be. The pendulum was swinging wildly. On the voyage back to New York, north through the tropical waters that were his most potent symbol, on 27 April 1932 at noon, Hart Crane climbed on the stern railing of the SS *Orizaba* and jumped.

To many of his friends and contemporaries, his suicide seemed an admonitory outcome – the consequence of unrestrained romanticism and a life given over too much to the pursuit of inspiration through extreme behaviour and emotional self-harm. But poems are in a sense composed anonymously – as much the product of tradition and the possibilities of language at a given time, as they are an expression of the individual ego. Crane would have assented to this view: he was dismayed only by his 'failure' to realise the visionary power of poetry to transform an intolerable world. I read him by chance at nineteen, when a schoolfriend brought back a second-hand copy of his poems from New York. I knew nothing of Crane's life then, of New York and the excitement of the Jazz Age, or of the innovative, and dangerous, tendencies of 1920s aesthetics.

But I knew these poems were unlike anything else I'd read. And they are indeed a unique hybrid of the most exotic possibilities of the language and have, at their best, a burnished splendour and magnificence. A couple of years later I walked across the Brooklyn Bridge (hand-in-hand with a girlfriend) declaiming 'Voyages ii' – an experience which marked my own early surrender to Crane's extravagant poetry.

MAURICE RIORDAN

HART CRANE

Sunday Morning Apples
To William Sommer

The leaves will fall again sometime and fill
The fleece of nature with those purposes
That are your rich and faithful strength of line.

But now there are challenges to spring
In that ripe nude with head
                         reared
Into a realm of swords, her purple shadow
Bursting on the winter of the world
From whiteness that cries defiance to the snow.

A boy runs with a dog before the sun, straddling
Spontaneities that form their independent orbits,
Their own perennials of light
In the valley where you live
                    (called Brandywine).

I have seen the apples there that toss you secrets, –
Beloved apples of seasonable madness
That feed your inquiries with aerial wine.

Put them again beside a pitcher with a knife,
And poise them full and ready for explosion –
The apples, Bill, the apples!

My Grandmother's Love Letters

There are no stars to-night
But those of memory.
Yet how much room for memory there is
In the loose girdle of soft rain.

There is even room enough
For the letters of my mother's mother,
Elizabeth,
That have been pressed so long
Into a corner of the roof
That they are brown and soft,
And liable to melt as snow.

Over the greatness of such space
Steps must be gentle.
It is all hung by an invisible white hair.
It trembles as birch limbs webbing the air.

And I ask myself:

'Are your fingers long enough to play
Old keys that are but echoes:
Is the silence strong enough
To carry back the music to its source
And back to you again
As though to her?'

Yet I would lead my grandmother by the hand
Through much of what she would not understand;
And so I stumble. And the rain continues on the roof
With such a sound of gently pitying laughter.

Episode of Hands

The unexpected interest made him flush.
Suddenly he seemed to forget the pain, –
Consented, – and held out
One finger from the others.

The gash was bleeding, and a shaft of sun
That glittered in and out among the wheels,
Fell lightly, warmly, down into the wound.

And as the fingers of the factory owner's son,
That knew a grip for books and tennis
As well as one for iron and leather, –
As his taut, spare fingers wound the gauze
Around the thick bed of the wound,
His own hands seemed to him
Like wings of butterflies
Flickering in sunlight over summer fields.

The knots and notches, – many in the wide
Deep hand that lay in his, – seemed beautiful.
They were like the marks of wild ponies' play, –
Bunches of new green breaking a hard turf.

And factory sounds and factory thoughts
Were banished from him by that larger, quieter hand
That lay in his with the sun upon it.
And as the bandage knot was tightened
The two men smiled into each other's eyes.

Chaplinesque

We make our meek adjustments,
Contented with such random consolations
As the wind deposits
In slithered and too ample pockets.

For we can still love the world, who find
A famished kitten on the step, and know
Recesses for it from the fury of the street,
Or warm torn elbow coverts.

We will sidestep, and to the final smirk
Dally the doom of that inevitable thumb
That slowly chafes its puckered index toward us,
Facing the dull squint with what innocence
And what surprise!

And yet these fine collapses are not lies
More than the pirouettes of any pliant cane;
Our obsequies are, in a way, no enterprise.
We can evade you, and all else but the heart:
What blame to us if the heart live on.

The game enforces smirks; but we have seen
The moon in lonely alleys make
A grail of laughter of an empty ash can,
And through all sound of gaiety and quest
Have heard a kitten in the wilderness.

Praise for an Urn
In Memoriam: Ernest Nelson

It was a kind and northern face
That mingled in such exile guise
The everlasting eyes of Pierrot
And, of Gargantua, the laughter.

His thoughts, delivered to me
From the white coverlet and pillow,
I see now, were inheritances –
Delicate riders of the storm.

The slant moon on the slanting hill
Once moved us toward presentiments
Of what the dead keep, living still,
And such assessments of the soul

As, perched in the crematory lobby,
The insistent clock commented on,
Touching as well upon our praise
Of glories proper to the time.

Still, having in mind gold hair,
I cannot see that broken brow
And miss the dry sound of bees
Stretching across a lucid space.

Scatter these well-meant idioms
Into the smoky spring that fills
The suburbs, where they will be lost.
They are no trophies of the sun.

Repose of Rivers

The willows carried a slow sound,
A sarabande the wind mowed on the mead.
I could never remember
That seething, steady leveling of the marshes
Till age had brought me to the sea.

Flags, weeds. And remembrance of steep alcoves
Where cypresses shared the noon's
Tyranny; they drew me into hades almost.
And mammoth turtles climbing sulphur dreams
Yielded, while sun-silt rippled them
Asunder . . .

How much I would have bartered! the black gorge
And all the singular nestings in the hills
Where beavers learn stitch and tooth.
The pond I entered once and quickly fled –
I remember now its singing willow rim.

And finally, in that memory all things nurse;
After the city that I finally passed
With scalding unguents spread and smoking darts
The monsoon cut across the delta
At gulf gates . . . There, beyond the dykes

I heard wind flaking sapphire, like this summer,
And willows could not hold more steady sound.

Passage

Where the cedar leaf divides the sky
I heard the sea.
In sapphire arenas of the hills
I was promised an improved infancy.

Sulking, sanctioning the sun,
My memory I left in a ravine, –
Casual louse that tissues the buckwheat,
Aprons rocks, congregates pears
In moonlit bushels
And wakens alleys with a hidden cough.

Dangerously the summer burned
(I had joined the entrainments of the wind).
The shadows of boulders lengthened my back:
In the bronze gongs of my cheeks
The rain dried without odour.

'It is not long, it is not long;
See where the red and black
Vine-stanchioned valleys –': but the wind
Died speaking through the ages that you know
And hug, chimney-sooted heart of man!
So was I turned about and back, much as your smoke
Compiles a too well-known biography.

The evening was a spear in the ravine
That throve through very oak. And had I walked
The dozen particular decimals of time?
Touching an opening laurel, I found
A thief beneath, my stolen book in hand.

'Why are you back here – smiling an iron coffin?'
'To argue with the laurel,' I replied:

'Am justified in transience, fleeing
Under the constant wonder of your eyes –.'

He closed the book. And from the Ptolemies
Sand troughed us in a glittering abyss.
A serpent swam a vertex to the sun
– On unpaced beaches leaned its tongue and drummed.
What fountains did I hear? what icy speeches?
Memory, committed to the page, had broke.

from The Marriage of Faustus and Helen

And yet, suppose some evening I forgot
The fare and transfer, yet got by that way
Without recall, – lost yet poised in traffic.
Then I might find your eyes across an aisle,
Still flickering with those prefigurations –
Prodigal, yet uncontested now,
Half-riant before the jerky window frame.

There is some way, I think, to touch
Those hands of yours that count the nights
Stippled with pink and green advertisements.
And now, before its arteries turn dark
I would have you meet this bartered blood.
Imminent in his dream, none better knows
The white wafer cheek of love, or offers words
Lightly as moonlight on the eaves meets snow.

Reflective conversion of all things
At your deep blush, when ecstasies thread
The limbs and belly, when rainbows spread
Impinging on the throat and sides . . .
Inevitable, the body of the world
Weeps in inventive dust for the hiatus
That winks above it, bluet in your breasts.

The earth may glide diaphanous to death;
But if I lift my arms it is to bend
To you who turned away once, Helen, knowing
The press of troubled hands, too alternate
With steel and soil to hold you endlessly.
I meet you, therefore, in that eventual flame
You found in final chains, no captive then –
Beyond their million brittle, bloodshot eyes;

White, through white cities passed on to assume
That world which comes to each of us alone.

Accept a lone eye riveted to your plane,
Bent axle of devotion along companion ways
That beat, continuous, to hourless days –
One inconspicuous, glowing orb of praise.

At Melville's Tomb

Often beneath the wave, wide from this ledge
The dice of drowned men's bones he saw bequeath
An embassy. Their numbers as he watched,
Beat on the dusty shore and were obscured.

And wrecks passed without sound of bells,
The calyx of death's bounty giving back
A scattered chapter, livid hieroglyph,
The portent wound in corridors of shells.

Then in the circuit calm of one vast coil,
Its lashings charmed and malice reconciled,
Frosted eyes there were that lifted altars;
And silent answers crept across the stars.

Compass, quadrant and sextant contrive
No farther tides . . . High in the azure steeps
Monody shall not wake the mariner.
This fabulous shadow only the sea keeps.

Voyages

II

– And yet this great wink of eternity,
Of rimless floods, unfettered leewardings,
Samite sheeted and processioned where
Her undinal vast belly moonward bends,
Laughing the wrapt inflections of our love;

Take this Sea, whose diapason knells
On scrolls of silver snowy sentences,
The sceptred terror of whose sessions rends
As her demeanors motion well or ill,
All but the pieties of lovers' hands.

And onward, as bells off San Salvador
Salute the crocus lustres of the stars,
In these poinsettia meadows of her tides, –
Adagios of islands, O my Prodigal,
Complete the dark confessions her veins spell.

Mark how her turning shoulders wind the hours,
And hasten while her penniless rich palms
Pass superscription of bent foam and wave, –
Hasten, while they are true, – sleep, death, desire,
Close round one instant in one floating flower.

Bind us in time, O Seasons clear, and awe.
O minstrel galleons of Carib fire,
Bequeath us to no earthly shore until
Is answered in the vortex of our grave
The seal's wide spindrift gaze toward paradise.

V

Meticulous, past midnight in clear rime,
Infrangible and lonely, smooth as though cast

Together in one merciless white blade –
The bay estuaries fleck the hard sky limits.

– As if too brittle or too clear to touch!
The cables of our sleep so swiftly filed,
Already hang, shred ends from remembered stars.
One frozen trackless smile . . . What words
Can strangle this deaf moonlight? For we

Are overtaken. Now no cry, no sword
Can fasten or deflect this tidal wedge,
Slow tyranny of moonlight, moonlight loved
And changed . . . 'There's

Nothing like this in the world,' you say,
Knowing I cannot touch your hand and look
Too, into that godless cleft of sky
Where nothing turns but dead sands flashing.

'– And never to quite understand!' No,
In all the argosy of your bright hair I dreamed
Nothing so flagless as this piracy.

                              But now
Draw in your head, alone and too tall here.
Your eyes already in the slant of drifting foam;
Your breath sealed by the ghosts I do not know:
Draw in your head and sleep the long way home.

VI

Where icy and bright dungeons lift
Of swimmers their lost morning eyes,
And ocean rivers, churning, shift
Green borders under stranger skies,

Steadily as a shell secretes
Its beating leagues of monotone,
Or as many waters trough the sun's
Red kelson past the cape's wet stone;

O rivers mingling toward the sky
And harbor of the phœnix' breast —
My eyes pressed black against the prow,
— Thy derelict and blinded guest

Waiting, afire, what name, unspoke,
I cannot claim: let thy waves rear
More savage than the death of kings,
Some splintered garland for the seer.

Beyond siroccos harvesting
The solstice thunders, crept away,
Like a cliff swinging or a sail
Flung into April's inmost day —

Creation's blithe and petalled word
To the lounged goddess when she rose
Conceding dialogue with eyes
That smile unsearchable repose —

Still fervid covenant, Belle Isle,
— Unfolded floating dais before
Which rainbows twine continual hair —
Belle Isle, white echo of the oarl

The imaged Word, it is, that holds
Hushed willows anchored in its glow.
It is the unbetrayable reply
Whose accent no farewell can know.

To Brooklyn Bridge

How many dawns, chill from his rippling rest
The seagull's wings shall dip and pivot him,
Shedding white rings of tumult, building high
Over the chained bay waters Liberty –

Then, with inviolate curve, forsake our eyes
As apparitional as sails that cross
Some page of figures to be filed away;
– Till elevators drop us from our day . . .

I think of cinemas, panoramic sleights
With multitudes bent toward some flashing scene
Never disclosed, but hastened to again,
Foretold to other eyes on the same screen;

And Thee, across the harbor, silver-paced
As though the sun took step of thee, yet left
Some motion ever unspent in thy stride, –
Implicitly thy freedom staying thee!

Out of some subway scuttle, cell or loft
A bedlamite speeds to thy parapets,
Tilting there momently, shrill shirt ballooning,
A jest falls from the speechless caravan.

Down Wall, from girder into street noon leaks,
A rip-tooth of the sky's acetylene;
All afternoon the cloud-flown derricks turn . . .
Thy cables breathe the North Atlantic still.

And obscure as that heaven of the Jews,
Thy guerdon . . . Accolade thou dost bestow
Of anonymity time cannot raise:
Vibrant reprieve and pardon thou dost show.

O harp and altar, of the fury fused,
(How could mere toil align thy choiring strings!)
Terrific threshold of the prophet's pledge,
Prayer of pariah, and the lover's cry, –

Again the traffic lights that skim thy swift
Unfractioned idiom, immaculate sigh of stars,
Beading thy path – condense eternity:
And we have seen night lifted in thine arms.

Under thy shadow by the piers I waited;
Only in darkness is thy shadow clear.
The City's fiery parcels all undone,
Already snow submerges an iron year . . .

O Sleepless as the river under thee,
Vaulting the sea, the prairies' dreaming sod,
Unto us lowliest sometime sweep, descend
And of the curveship lend a myth to God.

from Ave Maria

O Thou who sleepest on Thyself, apart
Like ocean athwart lanes of death and birth,
And all the eddying breath between dost search
Cruelly with love thy parable of man, –
Inquisitor! incognizable Word
Of Eden and the enchained Sepulchre,
Into thy steep savannahs, burning blue,
Utter to loneliness the sail is true.

Who grindest oar, and arguing the mast
Subscribest holocaust of ships, O Thou
Within whose primal scan consummately
The glistening seignories of Ganges swim; –
Who sendest greeting by the corposant,
And Teneriffe's garnet – flamed it in a cloud,
Urging through night our passage to the Chan; –
Te Deum laudamus, for thy teeming span!

Of all that amplitude that time explores,
A needle in the sight, suspended north, –
Yielding by inference and discard, faith
And true appointment from the hidden shoal:
This disposition that thy night relates
From Moon to Saturn in one sapphire wheel:
The orbic wake of thy once whirling feet,
Elohim, still I hear thy sounding heel!

White toil of heaven's cordons, mustering
In holy rings all sails charged to the far
Hushed gleaming fields and pendant seething wheat
Of knowledge, – round thy brows unhooded now
– The kindled Crown! acceded of the poles
And biassed by full sails, meridians reel
Thy purpose – still one shore beyond desire!

The sea's green crying towers a-sway, Beyond

And kingdoms
                    naked in the
                                   trembling heart –
   Te Deum laudamus
                        O Thou Hand of Fire

from Powhatan's Daughter

*'– Pocahuntus, a well-featured but wanton yong girle . . . of the age
of eleven or twelve years, get the boyes forth with her into the market
place, and make them wheele, falling on their hands, turning their
heels upwards, whom she would followe, and wheele so herself, naked
as she was, all the fort over.'*

THE HARBOR DAWN

Insistently through sleep – a tide of voices –
They meet you listening midway in your dream,
The long, tired sounds, fog-insulated noises:
Gongs in white surplices, beshrouded wails,
Far strum of fog horns . . . signals dispersed in veils.

And then a truck will lumber past the wharves
As winch engines begin throbbing on some deck;
Or a drunken stevedore's howl and thud below
Comes echoing alley-upward through dim snow.

And if they take your sleep away sometimes
They give it back again. Soft sleeves of sound
Attend the darkling harbor, the pillowed bay;
Somewhere out there in blankness steam

Spills into steam, and wanders, washed away
– Flurried by keen fifings, eddied
Among distant chiming buoys – adrift. The sky,
Cool feathery fold, suspends, distills
This wavering slumber. . . . Slowly –
Immemorially the window, the half-covered chair
Ask nothing but this sheath of pallid air.

And you beside me, blessèd now while sirens
Sing to us, stealthily weave us into day –
Serenely now, before day claims our eyes
Your cool arms murmurously about me lay.

400 years and
more . . . or is
it from the
soundless shore
of sleep that
time

recalls you to
your love,
there in a
waking dream
to merge
your seed

While myriad snowy hands are clustering at the panes –
  your hands within my hands are deeds;
  my tongue upon your throat – singing
  arms close; eyes wide, undoubtful
            dark
                 drink the dawn –
  a forest shudders in your hair!

The window goes blond slowly. Frostily clears.
From Cyclopean towers across Manhattan waters
– Two – three bright window-eyes aglitter, disk
The sun, released – aloft with cold gulls hither.

The fog leans one last moment on the sill.
Under the mistletoe of dreams, a star –
As though to join us at some distant hill –
Turns in the waking west and goes to sleep.

– with whom?

Who is the woman with us in the dawn? . . . whose is the flesh our feet have moved upon?

Macadam, gun-grey as the tunny's belt,
Leaps from Far Rockaway to Golden Gate:
Listen! the miles a hurdy-gurdy grinds –
Down gold arpeggios mile on mile unwinds.

Times earlier, when you hurried off to school,
– It is the same hour though a later day –
You walked with Pizarro in a copybook,
And Cortes rode up, reining tautly in –
Firmly as coffee grips the taste, – and away!

There was Priscilla's cheek close in the wind,
And Captain Smith, all beard and certainty,
And Rip Van Winkle bowing by the way, –
'Is this Sleepy Hollow, friend –?' And he –

And Rip forgot the office hours,
and he forgot the pay;
Van Winkle sweeps a tenement
way down on Avenue A, –

The grind-organ says . . . Remember, remember
The cinder pile at the end of the backyard
Where we stoned the family of young
Garter snakes under . . . And the monoplanes
We launched – with paper wings and twisted
Rubber bands . . . Recall – recall

*Streets spread
past store and
factory – sped
by sunlight
and her
smile . . .*

*Like Memory,
she is time's
truant, shall
take you by t
he hand . . .*

                              the rapid tongues
That flittered from under the ash heap day
After day whenever your stick discovered
Some sunning inch of unsuspecting fibre –
It flashed back at your thrust, as clean as fire.

And Rip was slowly made aware
          that he, Van Winkle, was not here
   nor there. He woke and swore he'd seen Broadway
          a Catskill daisy chain in May –

So memory, that strikes a rhyme out of a box,
Or splits a random smell of flowers through glass –
Is it the whip stripped from the lilac tree
One day in spring my father took to me,
Or is it the Sabbatical, unconscious smile
My mother almost brought me once from church
And once only, as I recall –?

It flickered through the snow screen, blindly
It forsook her at the doorway, it was gone
Before I had left the window. It
Did not return with the kiss in the hall.

Macadam, gun-grey as the tunny's belt,
Leaps from Far Rockaway to Golden Gate . . . .
Keep hold of that nickel for car-change, Rip, –
Have you got your '*Times*' –?
And hurry along, Van Winkle – it's getting late!

Stick your patent name on a signboard
brother – all over – going west – young man
Tintex – Japalac – Certain-teed Overalls ads
and lands sakes! under the new playbill ripped
in the guaranteed corner – see Bert Williams what?
Minstrels when you steal a chicken just
save me the wing for if it isn't
Erie it ain't for miles around a
Mazda – and the telegraphic night coming on Thomas

a Ediford – and whistling down the tracks
a headlight rushing with the sound – can you
imagine – while an EXPRESS makes time like
SCIENCE – COMMERCE and the HOLYGHOST
RADIO ROARS IN EVERY HOME WE HAVE THE NORTHPOLE
WALLSTREET AND VIRGINBIRTH WITHOUT STONES OR
WIRES OR EVEN RUNning brooks connecting ears
and no more sermons windows flashing roar
breathtaking – as you like it . . . eh?

        So the 20th Century – so
whizzed the Limited – roared by and left
three men, still hungry on the tracks, ploddingly
watching the tail lights wizen and converge, slip-
ping gimleted and neatly out of sight.

*

The last bear, shot drinking in the Dakotas
Loped under wires that span the mountain stream.

. . . and past
the din and
slogans of
the year –

Keen instruments, strung to a vast precision
Bind town to town and dream to ticking dream.
But some men take their liquor slow – and count
– Though they'll confess no rosary nor clue –
The river's minute by the far brook's year.
Under a world of whistles, wires and steam
Caboose-like they go ruminating through
Ohio, Indiana – blind baggage –
To Cheyenne tagging . . . Maybe Kalamazoo.

Time's rendings, time's blendings they construe
As final reckonings of fire and snow;
Strange bird-wit, like the elemental gist
Of unwalled winds they offer, singing low
My Old Kentucky Home and *Casey Jones*,
Some Sunny Day. I heard a road-gang chanting so.
And afterwards, who had a colt's eyes – one said,
'Jesus! Oh I remember watermelon days!' And sped
High in a cloud of merriment, recalled
'– And when my Aunt Sally Simpson smiled,' he
          drawled –
'It was almost Louisiana, long ago.'
'There's no place like Booneville though, Buddy,'
One said, excising a last burr from his vest,
'– For early trouting.' Then peering in the can,
'– But I kept on the tracks.' Possessed, resigned,
He trod the fire down pensively and grinned,
Spreading dry shingles of a beard. . . .

                                   Behind
My father's cannery works I used to see
Rail-squatters ranged in nomad raillery,
The ancient men – wifeless or runaway
Hobo-trekkers that forever search
An empire wilderness of freight and rails.

to those
whose addresses
are never near

Each seemed a child, like me, on a loose perch,
Holding to childhood like some termless play.
John, Jake or Charley, hopping the slow freight
– Memphis to Tallahassee – riding the rods,
Blind fists of nothing, humpty-dumpty clods.

Yet they touch something like a key perhaps.
From pole to pole across the hills, the states
– They know a body under the wide rain;
Youngsters with eyes like fjords, old reprobates
With racetrack jargon, – dotting immensity
They lurk across her, knowing her yonder breast
Snow-silvered, sumac-stained or smoky blue –
Is past the valley-sleepers, south or west.
– As I have trod the rumorous midnights, too,

And past the circuit of the lamp's thin flame
(O Nights that brought me to her body bare!)
Have dreamed beyond the print that bound her name.
Trains sounding the long blizzards out – I heard
Wail into distances I knew were hers.
Papooses crying on the wind's long mane
Screamed redskin dynasties that fled the brain,
– Dead echoes! But I knew her body there,
Time like a serpent down her shoulder, dark,
And space, an eaglet's wing, laid on her hair.

Under the Ozarks, domed by Iron Mountain,
The old gods of the rain lie wrapped in pools
Where eyeless fish curvet a sunken fountain
And re-descend with corn from querulous crows.
Such pilferings make up their timeless eatage,
Propitiate them for their timber torn
By iron, iron – always the iron dealt cleavage!
They doze now, below axe and powder horn.

but who have
touched her,
knowing her
without name

nor the
myths of her
fathers . . .

And Pullman breakfasters glide glistening steel
From tunnel into field – iron strides the dew –
Straddles the hill, a dance of wheel on wheel.
You have a half-hour's wait at Siskiyou,
Or stay the night and take the next train through.
Southward, near Cairo passing, you can see
The Ohio merging, – borne down Tennessee;
And if it's summer and the sun's in dusk
Maybe the breeze will lift the River's musk
– As though the waters breathed that you might know
Memphis Johnny, Steamboat Bill, Missouri Joe.
Oh, lean from the window, if the train slows down,
As though you touched hands with some ancient clown,
– A little while gaze absently below
And hum *Deep River* with them while they go.

Yes, turn again and sniff once more – look see,
O Sheriff, Brakeman and Authority –
Hitch up your pants and crunch another quid,
For you, too, feed the River timelessly.
And few evade full measure of their fate;
Always they smile out eerily what they seem.
I could believe he joked at heaven's gate –
Dan Midland – jolted from the cold brake-beam.

Down, down – born pioneers in time's despite,
Grimed tributaries to an ancient flow –
They win no frontier by their wayward plight,
But drift in stillness, as from Jordan's brow.

You will not hear it as the sea; even stone
Is not more hushed by gravity . . . But slow,
As loth to take more tribute – sliding prone
Like one whose eyes were buried long ago

The River, spreading, flows – and spends your dream.
What are you, lost within this tideless spell?
You are your father's father, and the stream –
A liquid theme that floating niggers swell.

Damp tonnage and alluvial march of days –
Nights turbid, vascular with silted shale
And roots surrendered down of moraine clays:
The Mississippi drinks the farthest dale.

O quarrying passion, undertowed sunlight!
The basalt surface drags a jungle grace
Ochreous and lynx-barred in lengthening might;
Patience! and you shall reach the biding place!

Over De Soto's bones the freighted floors
Throb past the City storied of three thrones.
Down two more turns the Mississippi pours
(Anon tall ironsides up from salt lagoons)

And flows within itself, heaps itself free.
All fades but one thin skyline 'round . . . Ahead
No embrace opens but the stinging sea;
The River lifts itself from its long bed,

Poised wholly on its dream, a mustard glow
Tortured with history, its one will – flow!
– The Passion spreads in wide tongues, choked and slow,
Meeting the Gulf, hosannas silently below.

The swift red flesh, a winter king –
Who squired the glacier woman down the sky?
She ran the neighing canyons all the spring;
She spouted arms; she rose with maize – to die.

And in the autumn drouth, whose burnished hands
With mineral wariness found out the stone
Where prayers, forgotten, streamed the mesa sands?
He holds the twilight's dim, perpetual throne.

Mythical brows we saw retiring – loth,
Disturbed and destined, into denser green.
Greeting they sped us, on the arrow's oath:
Now lie incorrigibly what years between . . .

There was a bed of leaves, and broken play;
There was a veil upon you, Pocahontas, bride –
O Princess whose brown lap was virgin May;
And bridal flanks and eyes hid tawny pride.

I left the village for dogwood. By the canoe
Tugging below the mill-race, I could see
Your hair's keen crescent running, and the blue
First moth of evening take wing stealthily.

What laughing chains the water wove and threw!
I learned to catch the trout's moon whisper; I
Drifted how many hours I never knew,
But, watching, saw that fleet young crescent die, –

And one star, swinging, take its place, alone,
Cupped in the larches of the mountain pass –
Until, immortally, it bled into the dawn.
I left my sleek boat nibbling margin grass . . .

*Then you shall
see her truly
– your blood
remembering
its first
invasion of her
secrecy, its
first encounters
with her kin,
her chieftain
lover . . . his
shade that
haunts the
lakes and hills*

I took the portage climb, then chose
A further valley-shed; I could not stop.
Feet nozzled wat'ry webs of upper flows;
One white veil gusted from the very top.

O Appalachian Spring! I gained the ledge;
Steep, inaccessible smile that eastward bends
And northward reaches in that violet wedge
Of Adirondacks! – wisped of azure wands,

Over how many bluffs, tarns, streams I sped!
– And knew myself within some boding shade:–
Grey tepees tufting the blue knolls ahead,
Smoke swirling through the yellow chestnut glade . . .

A distant cloud, a thunder-bud – it grew,
That blanket of the skies: the padded foot
Within, – I heard it; 'til its rhythm drew,
– Siphoned the black pool from the heart's hot root!

A cyclone threshes in the turbine crest,
Swooping in eagle feathers down your back;
Know, Maquokeeta, greeting; know death's best;
– Fall, Sachem, strictly as the tamarack!

A birch kneels. All her whistling fingers fly.
The oak grove circles in a crash of leaves;
The long moan of a dance is in the sky.
Dance, Maquokeeta: Pocahontas grieves . . .

And every tendon scurries toward the twangs
Of lightning deltaed down your saber hair.
Now snaps the flint in every tooth; red fangs
And splay tongues thinly busy the blue air . . .

Dance, Maquokeeta! snake that lives before,
That casts his pelt, and lives beyond! Sprout, horn!
Spark, tooth! Medicine-man, relent, restore –
Lie to us, – dance us back the tribal morn!

Spears and assemblies: black drums thrusting on –
O yelling battlements, – I, too, was liege
To rainbows currying each pulsant bone:
Surpassed the circumstance, danced out the siege!

And buzzard-circleted, screamed from the stake;
I could not pick the arrows from my side.
Wrapped in that fire, I saw more escorts wake –
Flickering, sprint up the hill groins like a tide.

I heard the hush of lava wrestling your arms,
And stag teeth foam about the raven throat;
Flame cataracts of heaven in seething swarms
Fed down your anklets to the sunset's moat.

O, like the lizard in the furious noon,
That drops his legs and colors in the sun,
– And laughs, pure serpent, Time itself, and moon
Of his own fate, I saw thy change begun!

And saw thee dive to kiss that destiny
Like one white meteor, sacrosanct and blent
At last with all that's consummate and free
There, where the first and last gods keep thy tent.

*

Thewed of the levin, thunder-shod and lean,
Lo, through what infinite seasons dost thou gaze –
Across what bivouacs of thine angered slain,
And see'st thy bride immortal in the maize!

Totem and fire-gall, slumbering pyramid –
Though other calendars now stack the sky,
Thy freedom is her largesse, Prince, and hid
On paths thou knewest best to claim her by.

High unto Labrador the sun strikes free
Her speechless dream of snow, and stirred again,
She is the torrent and the singing tree;
And she is virgin to the last of men . . .

West, west and south! winds over Cumberland
And winds across the llano grass resume
Her hair's warm sibilance. Her breasts are fanned
O stream by slope and vineyard – into bloom!

And when the caribou slant down for salt
Do arrows thirst and leap? Do antlers shine
Alert, star-triggered in the listening vault
Of dusk? – And are her perfect brows to thine?

We danced, O Brave, we danced beyond their farms,
In cobalt desert closures made our vows . . .
Now is the strong prayer folded in thine arms,
The serpent with the eagle in the boughs.

Cutty Sark

O, the navies old and oaken,
O, the Temeraire no more!
                    — MELVILLE

I met a man in South Street, tall –
a nervous shark tooth swung on his chain.
His eyes pressed through green grass
– green glasses, or bar lights made them
so –
    shine –
         GREEN –
                 eyes –
stepped out – forgot to look at you
or left you several blocks away –

in the nickel-in-the-slot piano jogged
'Stamboul Nights' – weaving somebody's nickel –
    sang –

  O Stamboul Rose – dreams weave the rose!

  Murmurs of Leviathan he spoke,
  and rum was Plato in our heads . . .

'It's S.S. *Ala* – Antwerp – now remember kid
to put me out at three she sails on time.
I'm not much good at time any more keep
weakeyed watches sometimes snooze –' his bony hands
got to beating time . . . 'A whaler once –
I ought to keep time and get over it – I'm a
Democrat – I know what time it is – No
I don't want to know what time it is – that
damned white Arctic killed my time . . .'

  O Stamboul Rose – dreams weave –

'I ran a donkey engine down there on the Canal
in Panama – got tired of that –
then Yucatan selling kitchenware – beads –
have you seen Popocatepetl – birdless mouth
with ashes sifting down –?
                              and then the coast again . . .'

Rose of Stamboul O coral Queen –
teased remnants of the skeletons of cities –
and galleries, galleries of watergutted lava
snarling stone – green – drums – drown –

Sing!
'– that spiracle!' he shot a finger out the door . . .
'O life's a geyser – beautiful – my lungs –
No – I can't live on land –!'

I saw the frontiers gleaming of his mind;
or are there frontiers – running sands sometimes
running sands – somewhere – sands running . . .
Or they may start some white machine that sings.
Then you may laugh and dance the axletree –
steel – silver – kick the traces – and know –

ATLANTIS ROSE drums wreathe the rose,
the star floats burning in a gulf of tears
and sleep another thousand –

                              interminably
long since somebody's nickel – stopped –
playing –

A wind worried those wicker-neat lapels, the
swinging summer entrances to cooler hells . . .
Outside a wharf truck nearly ran him down
– he lunged up Bowery way while the dawn
was putting the Statue of Liberty out – that
torch of hers you know –

I started walking home across the Bridge . . .

    *

Blithe Yankee vanities, turreted sprites, winged
                             British repartees, skil-
ful savage sea-girls
that bloomed in the spring – Heave, weave
those bright designs the trade winds drive . . .

> *Sweet opium and tea, Yo-ho!*
> *Pennies for porpoises that bank the keel!*
> *Fins whip the breeze around Japan!*

Bright skysails ticketing the Line, wink round the Horn
to Frisco, Melbourne . . .
                        Pennants, parabolas –
clipper dreams indelible and ranging,
baronial white on lucky blue!

> Perennial-*Cutty*-trophied-*Sark!*

Thermopylæ, Black Prince, Flying Cloud through Sunda
– scarfed of foam, their bellies veered green esplanades,
locked in wind-humors, ran their eastings down;

> *at Java Head freshened the nip*
> *(sweet opium and tea!)*
> *and turned and left us on the lee . . .*

Buntlines tusseling (91 days, 20 hours and anchored!)
                              Rainbow, Leander
(last trip a tragedy) – where can you be
Nimbus? and you rivals two –

           a long tack keeping –

                   Taeping?
                   Ariel?

from Three Songs

I wanted you, nameless Woman of the South,
No wraith, but utterly – as still more alone
The Southern Cross takes night
And lifts her girdles from her, one by one –
High, cool,
            wide from the slowly smoldering fire
Of lower heavens, –
                    vaporous scars!

Eve! Magdalene!
                or Mary, you?

Whatever call – falls vainly on the wave.
O simian Venus, homeless Eve,
Unwedded, stumbling gardenless to grieve
Windswept guitars on lonely decks forever;
Finally to answer all within one grave!

And this long wake of phosphor,
                            iridescent
Furrow of all our travel – trailed derision!
Eyes crumble at its kiss. Its long-drawn spell
Incites a yell. Slid on that backward vision
The mind is churned to spittle, whispering hell.

I wanted you . . . The embers of the Cross
Climbed by aslant and huddling aromatically.
It is blood to remember; it is fire
To stammer back . . . It is
God – your namelessness. And the wash –

All night the water combed you with black
Insolence. You crept out simmering, accomplished.

Water rattled that stinging coil, your
Rehearsed hair – docile, alas, from many arms.
Yes, Eve – wraith of my unloved seed!

The Cross, a phantom, buckled – dropped below the dawn.
Light drowned the lithic trillions of your spawn.

The Tunnel

To Find the Western path
Right thro' the Gates of Wrath.

— BLAKE

Performances, assortments, résumés —
Up Times Square to Columbus Circle lights
Channel the congresses, nightly sessions,
Refractions of the thousand theatres, faces —
Mysterious kitchens. . . . You shall search them all.
Someday by heart you'll learn each famous sight
And watch the curtain lift in hell's despite;
You'll find the garden in the third act dead,
Finger your knees — and wish yourself in bed
With tabloid crime-sheets perched in easy sight.

> Then let you reach your hat
> and go.
> As usual, let you — also
> walking down — exclaim
> to twelve upward leaving
> a subscription praise
> for what time slays.

Or can't you quite make up your mind to ride;
A walk is better underneath the L a brisk
Ten blocks or so before? But you find yourself
Preparing penguin flexions of the arms, —
As usual you will meet the scuttle yawn:
The subway yawns the quickest promise home.

Be minimum, then, to swim the hiving swarms
Out of the Square, the Circle burning bright —
Avoid the glass doors gyring at your right,
Where boxed alone a second, eyes take fright
— Quite unprepared rush naked back to light:

And down beside the turnstile press the coin
Into the slot. The gongs already rattle.

    And, so
    of cities you bespeak
    subways, rivered under streets
    and rivers. . . . In the car
    the overtone of motion
    underground, the monotone
    of motion is the sound
    of other faces, also underground –

'Let's have a pencil Jimmy – living now
at Floral Park
Flatbush – on the fourth of July –
like a pigeon's muddy dream – potatoes
to dig in the field – travlin the town – too –
night after night – the Culver line – the
girls all shaping up – it used to be –'

Our tongues recant like beaten weather vanes.
This answer lives like verdigris, like hair
Beyond extinction, surcease of the bone;
And repetition freezes – 'What

'what do you want? getting weak on the links?
fandaddle daddy don't ask for change – IS THIS
FOURTEENTH? it's half past six she said – if
you don't like my gate why did you
swing on it, why *didja*
swing on it
anyhow –'

    And somehow anyhow swing –

The phonographs of hades in the brain
Are tunnels that re-wind themselves, and love
A burnt match skating in a urinal –

Somewhere above Fourteenth TAKE THE EXPRESS
To brush some new presentiment of pain –

'But I want service in this office SERVICE
I said – after
the show she cried a little afterwards but –'

Whose head is swinging from the swollen strap?
Whose body smokes along the bitten rails,
Bursts from a smoldering bundle far behind
In back forks of the chasms of the brain, –
Puffs from a riven stump far out behind
In interborough fissures of the mind . . .?

And why do I often meet your visage here,
Your eyes like agate lanterns – on and on
Below the toothpaste and the dandruff ads?
– And did their riding eyes right through your side,
And did their eyes like unwashed platters ride?
And Death, aloft, – gigantically down
Probing through you – toward me, O evermore!
And when they dragged your retching flesh,
Your trembling hands that night through Baltimore –
That last night on the ballot rounds, did you
Shaking, did you deny the ticket, Poe?

For Gravesend Manor change at Chambers Street.
The platform hurries along to a dead stop.

The intent escalator lifts a serenade
Stilly
Of shoes, umbrellas, each eye attending its shoe, then
Bolting outright somewhere above where streets
Burst suddenly in rain. . . . The gongs recur:
Elbows and levers, guard and hissing door.
Thunder is galvothermic here below. . . . The car
Wheels off. The train rounds, bending to a scream,
Taking the final level for the dive

Under the river –
And somewhat emptier than before,
Demented, for a hitching second, humps; then
Lets go. . . . Toward corners of the floor
Newspapers wing, revolve and wing.
Blank windows gargle signals through the roar.

And does the Dæmon take you home, also,
Wop washerwoman, with the bandaged hair?
After the corridors are swept, the cuspidors –
The gaunt sky-barracks cleanly now, and bare,
O Genoese, do you bring mother eyes and hands
Back home to children and to golden hair?

Dæmon, demurring and eventful yawn!
Whose hideous laughter is a bellows mirth
– Or the muffled slaughter of a day in birth –
O cruelly to inoculate the brinking dawn
With antennæ toward worlds that glow and sink; –
To spoon us out more liquid than the dim
Locution of the eldest star, and pack
The conscience navelled in the plunging wind,
Umbilical to call – and straightway die!

O caught like pennies beneath soot and steam,
Kiss of our agony thou gatherest;
Condensed, thou takest all – shrill ganglia
Impassioned with some song we fail to keep.
And yet, like Lazarus, to feel the slope,
The sod and billow breaking, – lifting ground,
– A sound of waters bending astride the sky
Unceasing with some Word that will not die . . . !

       *

A tugboat, wheezing wreaths of steam,
Lunged past, with one galvanic blare stove up the River.
I counted the echoes assembling, one after one,
Searching, thumbing the midnight on the piers.

Lights, coasting, left the oily tympanum of waters;
The blackness somewhere gouged glass on a sky.
And this thy harbor, O my City, I have driven under,
Tossed from the coil of ticking towers. . . . Tomorrow,
And to be. . . . Here by the River that is East –
Here at the waters' edge the hands drop memory;
Shadowless in that abyss they unaccounting lie.
How far away the star has pooled the sea –
Or shall the hands be drawn away, to die?

Kiss of our agony Thou gatherest,
                    O Hand of Fire
                              gatherest –

Atlantis

*Music is then the knowledge of that which
relates to love in harmony and system.*

— PLATO

Through the bound cable strands, the arching path
Upward, veering with light, the flight of strings, –
Taut miles of shuttling moonlight syncopate
The whispered rush, telepathy of wires.
Up the index of night, granite and steel –
Transparent meshes – fleckless the gleaming staves –
Sibylline voices flicker, waveringly stream
As though a god were issue of the strings. . . .

And through that cordage, threading with its call
One arc synoptic of all tides below –
Their labyrinthine mouths of history
Pouring reply as though all ships at sea
Complighted in one vibrant breath made cry, –
'Make thy love sure – to weave whose song we ply!'
– From black embankments, moveless soundings hailed,
So seven oceans answer from their dream.

And on, obliquely up bright carrier bars
New octaves trestle the twin monoliths
Beyond whose frosted capes the moon bequeaths
Two worlds of sleep (O arching strands of song!) –
Onward and up the crystal-flooded aisle
White tempest nets file upward, upward ring
With silver terraces the humming spars,
The loft of vision, palladium helm of stars.

Sheerly the eyes, like seagulls stung with rime –
Slit and propelled by glistening fins of light –
Pick biting way up towering looms that press
Sidelong with flight of blade on tendon blade

– Tomorrows into yesteryear – and link
What cipher-script of time no traveller reads
But who, through smoking pyres of love and death,
Searches the timeless laugh of mythic spears.

Like hails, farewells – up planet-sequined heights
Some trillion whispering hammers glimmer Tyre:
Serenely, sharply up the long anvil cry
Of inchling æons silence rivets Troy.
And you, aloft there – Jason! hesting Shout!
Still wrapping harness to the swarming air!
Silvery the rushing wake, surpassing call,
Beams yelling Æolus! splintered in the straits!

From gulfs unfolding, terrible of drums,
Tall Vision-of-the-Voyage, tensely spare –
Bridge, lifting night to cycloramic crest
Of deepest day – O Choir, translating time
Into what multitudinous Verb the suns
And synergy of waters ever fuse, recast
In myriad syllables, – Psalm of Cathay!
O Love, thy white, pervasive Paradigm . . . !

We left the haven hanging in the night –
Sheened harbor lanterns backward fled the keel.
Pacific here at time's end, bearing corn, –
Eyes stammer through the pangs of dust and steel.
And still the circular, indubitable frieze
Of heaven's meditation, yoking wave
To kneeling wave, one song devoutly binds –
The vernal strophe chimes from deathless strings!

O Thou steeled Cognizance whose leap commits
The agile precincts of the lark's return;
Within whose lariat sweep encinctured sing
In single chrysalis the many twain, –
Of stars Thou art the stitch and stallion glow
And like an organ, Thou, with sound of doom –

Sight, sound and flesh Thou leadest from time's realm
As love strikes clear direction for the helm.

Swift peal of secular light, intrinsic Myth
Whose fell unshadow is death's utter wound, –
O River-throated – iridescently upborne
Through the bright drench and fabric of our veins;
With white escarpments swinging into light,
Sustained in tears the cities are endowed
And justified conclamant with ripe fields
Revolving through their harvests in sweet torment.

Forever Deity's glittering Pledge, O Thou
Whose canticle fresh chemistry assigns
To wrapt inception and beatitude, –
Always through blinding cables, to our joy,
Of thy white seizure springs the prophecy:
Always through spiring cordage, pyramids
Of silver sequel, Deity's young name
Kinetic of white choiring wings . . . ascends.

Migrations that must needs void memory,
Inventions that cobblestone the heart, –
Unspeakable Thou Bridge to Thee, O Love.
Thy pardon for this history, whitest Flower,
O Answerer of all, – Anemone, –
Now while thy petals spend the suns about us, hold –
(O Thou whose radiance doth inherit me)
Atlantis, – hold thy floating singer late!

So to thine Everpresence, beyond time,
Like spears ensanguined of one tolling star
That bleeds infinity – the orphic strings,
Sidereal phalanxes, leap and converge:
– One Song, one Bridge of Fire! Is it Cathay,
Now pity steeps the grass and rainbows ring
The serpent with the eagle in the leaves . . . ?
Whispers antiphonal in azure swing.

O Carib Isle!

The tarantula rattling at the lily's foot
Across the feet of the dead, laid in white sand
Near the coral beach – nor zigzag fiddle crabs
Side-stilting from the path (that shift, subvert
And anagrammatize your name) – No, nothing here
Below the palsy that one eucalyptus lifts
In wrinkled shadows – mourns.

                              And yet suppose
I count these nacreous frames of tropic death,
Brutal necklaces of shells around each grave
Squared off so carefully. Then

To the white sand I may speak a name, fertile
Albeit in a stranger tongue. Tree names, flower names
Deliberate, gainsay death's brittle crypt. Meanwhile
The wind that knots itself in one great death –
Coils and withdraws. So syllables want breath.

But where is the Captain of this doubloon isle
Without a turnstile? Who but catchword crabs
Patrols the dry groins of the underbrush?
What man, or What
Is Commissioner of mildew throughout the ambushed senses?
His Carib mathematics web the eyes' baked lenses!

Under the poinciana, of a noon or afternoon
Let fiery blossoms clot the light, render my ghost
Sieved upward, white and black along the air
Until it meets the blue's comedian host.

Let not the pilgrim see himself again
For slow evisceration bound like those huge terrapin
Each daybreak on the wharf, their brine-caked eyes;

– Spiked, overturned; such thunder in their strain!
And clenched beaks coughing for the surge again!

Slagged of the hurricane – I, cast within its flow,
Congeal by afternoons here, satin and vacant.
You have given me the shell, Satan, – carbonic amulet
Sere of the sun exploded in the sea.

The Air Plant
Grand Cayman

This tuft that thrives on saline nothingness,
Inverted octopus with heavenward arms
Thrust parching from a palm-bole hard by the cove –
A bird almost – of almost bird alarms,

Is pulmonary to the wind that jars
Its tentacles, horrific in their lurch.
The lizard's throat, held bloated for a fly,
Balloons but warily from this throbbing perch.

The needles and hack-saws of cactus bleed
A milk of earth when stricken off the stalk;
But this, – defenseless, thornless, sheds no blood,
Almost no shadow – but the air's thin talk.

Angelic Dynamo! Ventriloquist of the Blue!
While beachward creeps the shark-swept Spanish Main
By what conjunctions do the winds appoint
Its apotheosis, at last – the hurricane!

Key West

Here has my salient faith annealed me.
Out of the valley, past the ample crib
To skies impartial, that do not disown me
Nor claim me, either, by Adam's spine – nor rib.

The oar plash, and the meteorite's white arch
Concur with wrist and bicep. In the moon
That now has sunk I strike a single march
To heaven or hades – to an equally frugal noon.

Because these millions reap a dead conclusion
Need I presume the same fruit of my bone
As draws them towards a doubly mocked confusion
Of apish nightmares into steel-strung stone?

O, steel and stone! But gold was, scarcity before.
And here is water, and a little wind. . . .
There is no breath of friends and no more shore
Where gold has not been sold and conscience tinned.

Lenses

In the focus of the evening there is this island with the buzz of saw mills, the crunch and blast of quarries; furnaces, chisels and ploughs.

And the idiot boy by the road, with carbonated eyes, laughing or extending a phallus through the grating, – talking to a kite high in the afternoon, or in the twilight scanning pebbles among cinders in the road through a twice-opened tomato can.

And there is work, blood, suet and sweat, – the rigamarole of wine and mandolines. Midnight; and maybe love . . .

And there is, as Mr. Budge explained before his
chorea took him away – there is the Nine of
three-times-three, the hopeful plasm,
the vigilance of the ape, the repe-
tition of the parrot. Locks on
doors and lips of agony to
dance upon. And there is

time for these; time for all these, as cattle and birds
know, Mr.
Budge –
why did
you
die
so
soon
?

There is
this gate of
wrath

Bacardi Spreads the Eagle's Wings

'Pablo and Pedro, and black Serafin
Bought a launch last week. It might as well
Have been made of – well, say paraffin, –
That thin and blistered . . . just a rotten shell.

'Hell! out there among the barracudas
Their engine stalled, No oars, and leaks
Oozing a-plenty. They sat like baking Buddhas.
Luckily the Cayman schooner streaks

'By just in time, and lifts 'em high and dry . . .
They're back now on that mulching job at Pepper's.
– Yes, patent-leather shoes hot enough to fry
Anyone but these native high-steppers!'

Eternity

September – remember!
October – all over.
    — BARBADIAN ADAGE

After it was over, though still gusting balefully,
The old woman and I foraged some drier clothes
And left the house, or what was left of it;
Parts of the roof reached Yucatan, I suppose.
She almost – even then – got blown across lots
At the base of the mountain. But the town, the town!

Wires in the streets and Chinamen up and down
With arms in slings, plaster strewn dense with tiles,
And Cuban doctors, troopers, trucks, loose hens . . .
The only building not sagging on its knees,
Fernandez' Hotel, was requisitioned into pens
For cotted negroes, bandaged to be taken
To Havana on the first boat through. They groaned.

But was there a boat? By the wharf's old site you saw
Two decks unsandwiched, split sixty feet apart
And a funnel high and dry up near the park
Where a frantic peacock rummaged amid heaped cans.
No one seemed to be able to get a spark
From the world outside, but some rumor blew
That Havana, not to mention poor Batabanó,
Was halfway under water with fires
For some hours since – all wireless down
Of course, there too.

                    Back at the erstwhile house
We shoveled and sweated; watched the ogre sun
Blister the mountain, stripped now, bare of palm,
Everything – and lick the grass, as black as patent
Leather, which the rimed white wind had glazed.

Everything gone – or strewn in riddled grace –
Long tropic roots high in the air, like lace.
And somebody's mule steamed, swaying right by the pump,
Good God! as though his sinking carcass there
Were death predestined! You held your nose already
along the roads, begging for buzzards, vultures . . .
The mule stumbled, staggered. I somehow couldn't budge
To lift a stick for pity of his stupor.

                                            For I
Remember still that strange gratuity of horses
– One ours, and one, a stranger, creeping up with dawn
Out of the bamboo brake through howling, sheeted light
When the storm was dying. And Sarah saw them, too –
Sobbed. Yes, now – it's almost over. For they know;
The weather's in their noses. There's Don – but that one,
    white
– I can't account for him! And true, he stood
Like a vast phantom maned by all that memoried night
Of screaming rain – Eternity!

                                   Yet water, water!
I beat the dazed mule toward the road. He got that far
And fell dead or dying, but it didn't so much matter.
The morrow's dawn was dense with carrion hazes
Sliding everywhere. Bodies were rushed into graves
Without ceremony, while hammers pattered in town.
The roads were being cleared, injured brought in
And treated, it seemed. In due time
The President sent down a battleship that baked
Something like two thousand loaves on the way.
Doctors shot ahead from the deck in planes.
The fever was checked. I stood a long time in Mack's talking
New York with the gobs, Guantanamo, Norfolk, –
Drinking Bacardi and talking U.S.A.

A Postscript

Friendship agony! words came to me
at last shyly. My only final friends –
the wren and thrush, made solid print for me
across dawn's broken arc. No; yes . . . or were they
the audible ransom, ensign of my faith
toward something far, now farther than ever away?

Remember the lavender lilies of that dawn,
their ribbon miles, beside the railroad ties
as one nears New Orleans, sweet trenches by the train
after the western desert and the later cattle country;
and other gratuities, like porters' jokes, roses . . .

Dawn's broken arc! the noon's more furbished room!
Yet seldom was there faith in the heart's right kindness.
There were tickets and alarm clocks. There were counters and
    schedules;
and a paralytic woman on an island of the Indies,
Antillean fingers counting my pulse, my love forever.

The Broken Tower

The bell-rope that gathers God at dawn
Dispatches me as though I dropped down the knell
Of a spent day – to wander the cathedral lawn
From pit to crucifix, feet chill on steps from hell.

Have you not heard, have you not seen that corps
Of shadows in the tower, whose shoulders sway
Antiphonal carillons launched before
The stars are caught and hived in the sun's ray?

The bells, I say, the bells break down their tower;
And swing I know not where. Their tongues engrave
Membrane through marrow, my long-scattered score
Of broken intervals . . . And I, their sexton slave!

Oval encyclicals in canyons heaping
The impasse high with choir. Banked voices slain!
Pagodas, campaniles with reveilles outleaping –
O terraced echoes prostrate on the plain! . . .

And so it was I entered the broken world
To trace the visionary company of love, its voice
An instant in the wind (I know not whither hurled)
But not for long to hold each desperate choice.

My word I poured. But was it cognate, scored
Of that tribunal monarch of the air
Whose thigh embronzes earth, strikes crystal Word
In wounds pledged once to hope – cleft to despair?

The steep encroachments of my blood left me
No answer (could blood hold such a lofty tower
As flings the question true?) – or is it she
Whose sweet mortality stirs latent power? –

And through whose pulse I hear, counting the strokes
My veins recall and add, revived and sure
The angelus of wars my chest evokes:
What I hold healed, original now, and pure . . .

And builds, within, a tower that is not stone
(Not stone can jacket heaven) – but slip
Of pebbles, – visible wings of silence sown
In azure circles, widening as they dip

The matrix of the heart, lift down the eye
That shrines the quiet lake and swells a tower . . .
The commodious, tall decorum of that sky
Unseals her earth, and lifts love on its shower.

LETTERS

To William Wright – 17 October 1921

Dear William: I can come half way with you about Edna Millay, – but I fear not much further. She really has genius in a limited sense, and is much better than Sara Teasdale, Marguerite Wilkinson, Lady Speyer, etc., to mention a few drops in the bucket of feminine lushness that forms a kind of milky way in the poetic firmament of the time (likewise all times); – indeed I think she is every bit as good as Elizabeth Browning. And here it will be probably evident that most of her most earnest devotees could not ask for more. I can only say that I also do not greatly care for Mme. Browning. And on top of my dislike for this lady, Tennyson, Thompson, Chatterton, Byron, Moore, Milton, and several more, I have the apparent brassiness to call myself a person of rather catholic admirations. But you will also notice that I *do* run joyfully toward Messrs. Poe, Whitman, Shakespeare, Keats, Shelley, Coleridge, John Donne!!!, John Webster!!!, Marlowe, Baudelaire, Laforgue, Dante, Cavalcanti, Li Po, and a host of others. Oh I wish we had an evening to talk over poetic creeds, – it is ridiculous to attempt it in a letter. I can only apologize by saying that if my work seems needlessly sophisticated it is because I am only interested in adding what seems to me something really *new* to what *has* been written. Unless one has some new, intensely personal viewpoint to record, say on the eternal feelings of love, and the suitable personal idiom to employ in the act, I say, why write about it? Nine chances out of ten, if you know where in the past to look, you will find words already written in the more-or-less exact tongue of your soul. And the complaint to be made against nine out of ten poets is just this, – that you are apt to find their sentiments much better expressed perhaps four hundred years past. And it is not that Miss Millay fails entirely, but that I often am made to hear too many echoes in her things, that I cannot like her as well as you do. With her equipment Edna Millay is bound to succeed to the appreciative applause of a fairly large audience. And for you, who I rather suppose have not gone into this branch of literature with as much enthusiasm as myself, she is a creditable heroine.

I admit to a slight leaning toward the esoteric, and am perhaps not to be taken seriously. I am fond of things of great fragility, and also and especially of the kind of poetry John Donne represents, a dark musky, brooding, speculative vintage, at once sensual and spiritual, and singing rather the beauty of experience than innocence.

As you did not 'get' my idiom in 'Chaplinesque,' I feel rather like doing my best to explain myself. I am moved to put Chaplin with the poets (of today); hence the 'we.' In other words, he, especially in *The Kid*, made me feel myself, as a poet, as being 'in the same boat' with him. Poetry, the human feelings, 'the kitten,' is so crowded out of the humdrum, rushing, mechanical scramble of today that the man who would preserve them must duck and camouflage for dear life to keep them or keep himself from annihilation. I have since learned that I am by no means alone in seeing these things in the buffooneries of the tragedian, Chaplin, (if you want to read the opinions of the London and Paris presses, see *Literary Digest*, Oct. 8th) and in the poem I have tried to express these 'social sympathies' in words corresponding somewhat to the antics of the actor. I may have failed, as only a small number of those I have shown it to have responded with any clear answer, – but on the other hand, I realize that the audience for my work will always be quite small. I freely admit to a liking for the thing, myself, – in fact I have to like something of my own once in a while being so hard to please anyway. [. . .]

To Allen Tate – 12 June 1922

Dear Allen: So you are in love with the dear Duchess of Malfi also! How lovely she speaks in that one matchless passage: [*The Duchess of Malfi*, III, ii, 66–70]. Exquisite pride surrendering to love! And it was this that faced all the brutality of circumstance in those hideous and gorgeous final scenes of the play! The old betrayals of life, and yet they are worth something – from a distance, afterward.

What you say about Eliot does not surprise me, – but you will recover from the shock. No one ever says the last word, and it is a good thing for you, (notice how I congratulate myself!) to have been faced with him as early as possible. I have been facing him for *four* years, – and while I haven't discovered a weak spot yet in his armour, I flatter myself a little lately that I have discovered a safe tangent to strike which, if I can possibly explain the position, – goes *through* him toward a *different goal*. You see it is such a fearful temptation to imitate him that at times I have been almost distracted. He is, you have now discovered, far more profound than Huxley (whom I like) or any others obviously under his influence. You will profit by reading him again and again. I must have read 'Prufrock' twenty-five times and things like the 'Preludes' more often. His work will lead you back to some of the Elizabethans and point out the best in them. And there is Henry James, Laforgue, Blake and a dozen others in his work. He wrote most of this verse between 22 and 25, and is now, I understand, dying piecemeal as a clerk in a London bank! In his own realm Eliot presents us with an absolute *impasse*, yet oddly enough, he can be utilized to lead us to, intelligently point to, other positions and 'pastures new.' Having absorbed him enough we can trust ourselves as never before, in the air or on the sea. I, for instance, would like to leave a few of his 'negations' behind me, risk the realm of the obvious more, in quest of new sensations, *humeurs*. These theories and manoeuvres are interesting and consolatory, – but of course, when it comes right down to the act itself, – I have to depend on intuition, 'inspiration' or what you will to fill up the page. Let us not be too much disturbed, antagonized or influenced by the *fait accompli*. For in the words of our divine object of 'envy' ('Reflections on Contemporary Poetry,' *Egoist*, London, '19–): 'Admiration leads most often to imitation; we can seldom long remain unconscious of our imitating another, and the awareness of our imitation naturally leads us to hatred of the object imitated. [. . .]

To Gorham Munson – *c.* 18 June 1922

[. . .] At times, dear Gorham, I feel an enormous power in me – that seems almost supernatural. If this power is not too dissipated in aggravation and discouragement I may amount to something sometime. I can say this now with perfect equanimity because I am notoriously drunk and the Victrola is still going with that glorious 'Bolero.' Did I tell you of that thrilling experience this last winter in the dentist's chair when under the influence of aether and *amnesia* my mind spiraled to a kind of seventh heaven of consciousness and egoistic dance among the seven spheres – and something like an objective voice kept saying to me – 'You have the higher consciousness – you have the higher consciousness. This is something that very few have. This is what is called genius.'? A happiness, ecstatic such as I have known only twice in 'inspirations' came over me. I felt the two worlds. And at once. As the bore went into my tooth I was able to follow its every revolution as detached as a spectator at a funeral. O Gorham, I have known moments in eternity. I tell you this as one who is a brother. I want you to know me as I feel myself to be sometimes. I don't want you to feel that I am conceited. But since this adventure in the dentist's chair, I feel a new confidence in myself. At least I had none of the ordinary hallucinations common to this operation. Even that means something. You know I live for work, – for poetry. I shall do my best work later on when I am about 35 or 40. The imagination is the only thing worth a damn. [. . .]

To Gorham Munson – 5 January 1923

[. . .] There is no one writing in English who can command so much respect, to my mind, as Eliot. However, I take Eliot as a point of departure toward an almost complete reverse of direction. His pessimism is amply justified, in his own case. But I would apply as much of his erudition and technique as I can absorb and assemble toward a more positive, or (if [I] must put it so in a sceptical age) ecstatic goal. I should not think of this if a kind of rhythm and ecstasy were not (at odd moments, and rare!) a very real thing to me. I feel that Eliot ignores certain spiritual events and possibilities as real and powerful now as, say, in the time of Blake. Certainly the man has dug the ground and buried hope as deep and direfully as it can ever be done. [. . .]

To Gorham Munson – 18 February 1923

[. . .] I am too much interested in this *Bridge* thing lately to write letters, ads, or anything. It is just beginning to take the least outline, – and the more outline the conception of the thing takes, – the more its final difficulties appal me. All this preliminary thought has to result, of course, in some channel forms or mould into which I throw myself at white heat. Very roughly, it concerns a mystical synthesis of 'America.' History and fact, location, etc., all have to be transfigured into abstract form that would almost function independently of its subject matter. The initial impulses of 'our people' will have to be gathered up toward the climax of the bridge, symbol of our constructive future, our unique identity, in which is included also our scientific hopes and achievements of the future. The mystic portent of all this is already flocking through my mind (when I say this I should say 'the mystic possibilities,' but that is all that's worth announcing, anyway) but the actual statement of the thing, the marshalling of the forces, will take me months, at best; and I may have to give it up entirely before that; it may be too impossible an ambition. But if I do succeed, such a waving of banners, such ascent of towers, such dancing, etc., will never before have been put down on paper! [. . .]

To Waldo Frank – 21 April 1924

Dear Waldo: For many days, now, I have gone about quite dumb with something for which 'happiness' must be too mild a term. At any rate, my aptitude for communication, such as it ever is!, has been limited to one person alone, and perhaps for the first time in my life (and, I can only think that it is for the last, so far is my imagination from the conception of anything more profound and lovely than this love). I have wanted to write you more than once, but it will take many letters to let you know what I mean (for myself, at least) when I say that I have seen the Word made Flesh. I mean nothing less, and I know now that there is such a thing as indestructibility. In the deepest sense, where flesh became transformed through intensity of response to counter-response, where sex was beaten out, where a purity of joy was reached that included tears. It's true, Waldo, that so much more than my frustrations and multitude of humiliations has been answered in this reality and promise that I feel that whatever event the future holds is justified beforehand. And I have been able to give freedom and life which was acknowledged in the ecstasy of walking hand in hand across the most beautiful bridge of the world, the cables enclosing us and pulling us upward in such a dance as I have never walked and never can walk with another.

Note the above address [110 Columbia Heights], and you will see that I am living in the shadow of that bridge. It is so quiet here; in fact, it's like the moment of the communion with the 'religious gunman' in my 'F and H' where the edge of the bridge leaps over the edge of the street. It was in the evening darkness of its shadow that I started the last part of that poem. Imagine my surprise when Emil brought me to this street where, at the very end of it, I saw a scene that was more familiar than a hundred factual previsions could have rendered it! And there is all the glorious dance of the river directly beyond the back window of the room I am to have as soon as Emil's father moves out, which is to be soon. Emil will be back then from S. America where he had to ship for wages as ship's writer. That window is where I would be most remembered of all: the ships, the harbor, and the skyline of Manhattan, midnight, morning or evening, – rain, snow or sun, it is everything from mountains to the walls of Jerusalem and Nineveh, and all related and in actual contact with the changelessness of the many waters that surround it. I think the sea has thrown itself upon me and been answered, at least in part, and I believe I am a little changed – not essentially, but changed and transubstantiated as anyone is who has asked a question and been answered. [. . .]

To Waldo Frank – 20 June 1926

[. . .] The form of my poem rises out of a past that so over-whelms the present with its worth and vision that I'm at a loss to explain my delusion that there exist any real links between that past and a future destiny worthy of it. The 'destiny' is long since completed, perhaps the little last section of my poem is a hangover echo of it – but it hangs suspended somewhere in ether like an Absalom by his hair. The bridge as a symbol today has no signifi-cance beyond an economical approach to shorter hours, quicker lunches, behaviorism and toothpicks. And inasmuch as the bridge is a symbol of all such poetry as I am interested in writing it is my present fancy that a year from now I'll be more contented working in an office than before. Rimbaud was the last great poet that our civilization will see – he let off all the great cannon crackers in Valhalla's parapets, the sun has set theatrically sev-eral times since while Laforgue, Eliot and others of that kidney have whimpered fastidiously. *Everybody* writes poetry now – and 'poets' for the first time are about to receive official social and economic recognition in America. It's really all the fashion, but a dead bore to anticipate. If only America were half as worthy today to be spoken of as Whitman spoke of it fifty years ago there might be something for me to say – not that Whitman received or required any tangible proof of his intimations, but that time has shown how increasingly lonely and ineffectual his confidence stands [. . .]

To Waldo Frank – 19 August 1926

Dear Waldo: Here, too, is that bird with a note that Rimbaud speaks of as 'making you blush.' We are in the midst of the equatorial storm season; everyday, often at night, torrents engulf us, and the thunder rods jab and prospect in the caverns deep below that chain of mountains across. You can hear the very snakes rejoice, – the long, shaken-out convulsions of rock and roots.

It is very pleasant to lie awake – just half awake – and listen. I have the most speechless and glorious dreams meanwhile. Sometimes words come and go, presented like a rose that yields only its light, never its composite form. Then the cocks begin to crow. I hear Mrs. S – begin to stir. She is the very elf of music, little wrinkled burnous wisp that can do anything and remembers so much! She reads Dante and falls to sleep, her cough has become so admirably imitated by the parrot that I often think her two places at once. [. . .]

Yes, I read the whole of Spengler's book. It is stupendous, – and it was perhaps a very good experience for ripening some of *The Bridge*, after all. I can laugh now; but you know, alas, how little I could at the time. That book seems to have been just one more of many 'things' and circumstances that seem to have uniformly conspired in a strangely symbolical way toward the present speed of my work. Isn't it true – hasn't it been true in your experience, that beyond the acceptance of fate as a tragic action – immediately every circumstance and incident in one's life flocks toward a positive center of action, control and beauty? [. . .]

To Harriet Monroe – from *Poetry* 29 (October 1926)

Your good nature and manifest interest in writing me about the obscurities apparent in my Melville poem certainly prompt a wish to clarify my intentions in that poem as much as possible. But I realize that my explanations will not be very convincing.

For a paraphrase is generally a poor substitute for any organized conception that one has fancied he has put into the more essentialized form of the poem itself.

At any rate, and though I imagine us to have considerable differences of opinion regarding the relationship of poetic metaphor to ordinary logic (I judge this from the angle of approach you use toward portions of the poem), I hope my answers will not be taken as a defense of merely certain faulty lines. I am really much more interested in certain theories of metaphor and technique involved generally in poetics, than I am concerned in vindicating any particular perpetrations of my own.

My poem may well be elliptical and actually obscure in the ordering of its content, but in your criticism of this very possible deficiency you have stated your objections in terms that allow me, at least for the moment, the privilege of claiming your ideas and ideals as theoretically, at least, quite outside the issues of my own aspirations. To put it more plainly, as a poet I may very possibly be more interested in the so-called illogical impingements of the connotations of words on the consciousness (and their combinations and interplay in metaphor on this basis) than I am interested in the preservation of their logically rigid significations at the cost of limiting my subject matter and perceptions involved in the poem.

This may sound as though I merely fancied juggling words and images until I found something novel, or esoteric; but the process is much more predetermined and objectified than that. The nuances of feeling and observation in a poem may well call for certain liberties which you claim the poet has no right to take. I am simply making the claim that the poet does have that authority, and that to deny it is to limit the scope of the medium so considerably as to outlaw some of the richest genius of the past.

This argument over the dynamics of metaphor promises as active a future as has been evinced in the past. Partaking so extensively as it does of the issues involved in the propriety or non-propriety of certain attitudes toward subject matter, etc., it enters the critical distinctions usually made between 'romantic' [and] 'classic' as an organic factor. It is a problem that would require many pages to state adequately – merely from my own limited standpoint on the issues. Even this limited statement may prove onerous reading, and I hope you will pardon me if my own interest in the matter carries me to the point of presumption.

Its paradox, of course, is that its apparent illogic operates so logically in conjunction with its context in the poem as to establish its claim to another logic, quite independent of the original definition of the word or phrase or image thus employed. It implies (this *inflection* of language) a previous or prepared receptivity to its stimulus on the part of the reader. The reader's sensibility simply responds by identifying this inflection of experience with some event in his own history or perceptions – or rejects it altogether. The logic of metaphor is so organically entrenched in pure sensibility that it can't be thoroughly traced or explained outside of historical sciences, like philology and anthropology. This 'pseudo-statement,' as I. A. Richards calls it in an admirable essay touching our contentions in last July's *Criterion*, demands completely other faculties of recognition than the pure rationalistic associations permit. Much fine poetry may be completely rationalistic in its use of symbols, but there is much great poetry of another order which will yield the reader very little when inspected under the limitation of such arbitrary concerns as are manifested in your judgment of the Melville poem, especially when you constitute such requirements of ordinary logical relationship between word and word as irreducible.

I don't wish to enter here defense of the particular symbols employed in my own poem, because, as I said, I may well have failed to supply the necessary emotional connectives to the content featured. But I would like to counter a question or so of yours with a similar question. Here the poem is less dubious in quality than my own, and as far as the abstract pertinacity of question and its immediate consequences are concerned the point I'm arguing about can be better demonstrated. Both quotations are familiar to you, I'm sure.

You ask me how a *portent* can possibly be wound in a *shell*. Without attempting to answer this for the moment, I ask you how Blake could possibly say that 'a *sigh* is a *sword* of an Angel King.' You ask me how *compass, quadrant and sextant* '*contrive*' tides. I ask you how Eliot can possibly believe that 'Every street *lamp* that I pass *beats* like a fatalistic *drum!*' Both of my metaphors may fall down completely. I'm not defending their actual value in themselves; but your criticism of them in each case was leveled at an illogicality of relationship between symbols, which similar fault you must have either overlooked in case you have ever admired the Blake and Eliot lines, or have there condoned them on account of some more ultimate convictions pressed on you by the impact of the poems in their entirety.

It all comes to the recognition that emotional dynamics are not to be confused with any absolute order of rationalized definitions; ergo, in poetry the *rationale* of metaphor belongs to another order of experience than science, and is not to be limited by a scientific and arbitrary code of relationships either in verbal inflections or concepts.

There are plenty of people who have never accumulated a sufficient series of reflections (and these of a rather special nature) to perceive the relation between a *drum* and a *street lamp* – *via* the *unmentioned* throbbing of the heart and nerves in a distraught man which *tacitly* creates the reason and 'logic' of the Eliot metaphor. They will always have a perfect justification for ignoring those lines and to claim them obscure, excessive, etc., until by some experience of their own the words accumulate the necessary connotations to complete their connection. It is the same with the 'patient etherized upon a table,' isn't it? Surely that line must lack all eloquence to many people who, for instance, would delight in agreeing that the sky was like a dome of many-colored glass. [. . .]

Not to rant on forever, I'll beg your indulgence and come at

79

once to the explanations you requested on the Melville poem:

'The dice of drowned men's bones he saw bequeath

An embassy.'

Dice bequeath an embassy, in the first place, by being ground (in this connection only, of course) in little cubes from the bones of drowned men by the action of the sea, and are finally thrown up on the sand, having 'numbers' but no identification. These being the bones of dead men who never completed their voyage, it seems legitimate to refer to them as the only surviving evidence of certain messages undelivered, mute evidence of certain things, experiences that the dead mariners might have had to deliver. Dice as a symbol of chance and circumstance is also implied.

'The calyx of death's bounty giving back,' etc.

This calyx refers in a double ironic sense both to a cornucopia and the vortex made by a sinking vessel. As soon as the water has closed over a ship, this whirlpool sends up broken spars, wreckage, etc., which can be alluded to as livid *hieroglyphs*, making a *scattered chapter* so far as any complete record of the recent ship and her crew is concerned. In fact, about as much definite knowledge might come from all this as anyone might gain from the roar of his own veins, which is easily heard (haven't you ever done it?) by holding a shell close to one's ear.

'Frosted eyes lift altars.'

Refers simply to a conviction that a man, not knowing perhaps a definite god yet being endowed with a reverence for deity – such a man naturally postulates a deity somehow, and the altar of that deity by the very *action* of the eyes *lifted* in searching.

'Compass, quadrant and sextant contrive no farther tides.'

Hasn't it often occurred that instruments originally invented for record and computation have inadvertently so extended the concepts of the entity they were invented to measure (concepts of space, etc.) in the mind and imagination that employed them, that they may metaphorically be said to have extended the original boundaries of the entity measured? This little bit of 'relativity' ought not to be discredited in poetry now that scientists are proceeding to measure the universe on principles of pure *ratio*, quite as metaphorical, so far as previous standards of scientific methods extended, as some of the axioms in Job.

I may have completely failed to provide any clear interpretation of these symbols in their context. And you will no doubt feel that I have rather heatedly explained them for anyone who professes no claims for their particular value. I hope, at any rate, that I have clarified them enough to suppress any suspicion that their obscurity derives from a lack of definite intentions in the subject-matter of the poem. The execution is another matter, and you must be accorded a superior judgment to mine in that regard.

To Yvor Winters – 29 May 1927

Dear Winters: You need a good drubbing for all your recent easy talk about 'the complete man,' the poet and his ethical place in society, etc. I'm afraid I lack the time right now to attempt what I might call a relatively complete excuse for committing myself to the above sentiments – and I am also encumbered by a good deal of sympathy with your viewpoint in general. Wilson's article was just half-baked enough to make one warm around the collar. It is so damned easy for such as he, born into easy means, graduated from a fashionable university into a critical chair overlooking Washington Square, etc., to sit tight and hatch little squibs of advice to poets not to be so 'professional' as he claims they are, as though all the names he has just mentioned had been as suavely nourished as he – as though 4 out of 5 of them hadn't been damned well forced the major part of their lives to grub at *any* kind of work they could manage by hook or crook and the fear of hell to secure! Yes, why not step into the State Dept. and join the diplomatic corps for a change! indeed, or some other courtly occupation which would bring you into wide and active contact with world affairs! As a matter of fact I'm all too ready to concede that there are several other careers more engaging to follow than that of poetry. But the circumstances of one's birth, the conduct of one's parents, the current economic structure of society and a thousand other local factors have as much or more to say about successions to such occupations, the naive volitions of the poet to the contrary. I agree with you, of course, that the poet should in as large a measure as possible adjust himself to society. But the question always will remain as to how far the conscience is justified in compromising with the age's demands.

The image of 'the complete man' is a good idealistic antidote for the hysteria for specialization that inhabits the modern world. And I strongly second your wish for some definite ethical order. Munson, however, and a number of my other friends, not so long ago, being stricken with the same urge, and feeling that something must be done about it – rushed into the portals of the famous Gurdjieff Institute and have since put themselves through all sorts of Hindu antics, songs, dances, incantations, psychic sessions, etc., so that now, presumably the left lobes of their brains and their right lobes respectively function (M's favorite word) in perfect unison. I spent hours at the typewriter trying to explain to certain of these urgent people why I could not enthuse about their methods; it was all to no avail, as I was told that the 'complete man' had a different logic than mine, and further that there was no way of gaining or understanding this logic without first submitting yourself to the necessary training. I was finally left to roll in the gutter of my ancient predispositions, and suffered to receive a good deal of unnecessary pity for my obstinacy. Some of them, having found a good substitute for their former interest in writing by means of more complete formulas of expression have ceased writing altogether, which is probably just as well. At any rate they have become hermetically sealed souls to my eyesight, and I am really not able to offer judgment. [. . .]

You put me in altogether too good company, you compliment

me much too highly for me to offer the least resistance to your judgments on the structure of my work. I think I am quite unworthy of such associates as Marlowe or Valéry – except in some degree, perhaps, 'by kind.' If I can avoid the pearly gates long enough I may do better. Your fumigation of the Leonardo legend is a healthy enough reaction, but I don't think your reasons for doubting his intelligence and scope very potent. I've never closely studied the man's attainments or biography, but your argument is certainly weakly enough sustained on the sole prop of his sex – or lack of such. One doesn't have to turn to homosexuals to find instances of missing sensibilities. Of course I'm sick of all this talk about b—s and c—s in criticism. It's obvious that b—s are needed, and that Leonardo had 'em – at least the records of the Florentine prisons, I'm told, say so. You don't seem to realize that the whole topic is something of a myth anyway, and is consequently modified in the characteristics of the image by each age in each civilization. Tom Jones, a character for whom I have the utmost affection, represented the model in 18th Century England, at least so far as the stated requirements in your letter would suggest, and for an Anglo-Saxon model he is still pretty good aside from calculus, the Darwinian theory, and a few other mental additions. Incidentally I think Tom Jones (Fielding himself, of course) represents a much more 'balanced' attitude toward society and life in general than our friend, Thomas Hardy. Hardy's profundity is real, but it is voiced in pretty much one monotonous key. I think him perhaps the greatest technician in English verse since Shakespeare. He's a great poet and a mighty man. But you must be fanatic to feel that he fulfills the necessary 'balanced ration' for modern consumption. Not one of his characters is for one moment allowed to express a single joyous passion without a forenote of Hardian doom entering the immediate description. Could Hardy create anything like Falstaff? I think that Yeats would be just as likely – more so.

That's what I'm getting at. . . . I don't care to be credited with too wholesale ambitions, for as I said, I realize my limitations, and have already partially furled my flag. The structural weaknesses which you find in my work are probably quite real, for I could not ask for a more meticulous and sensitive reader. It is my hope, of course, not only to improve my statement but to extend scope and viewpoint as much as possible. But I cannot trust to so methodical and predetermined a method of development, not by any means, as you recommend. Nor can I willingly permit you to preserve the assumption that I am seeking any 'shortcuts across the circle,' nor wilfully excluding any experience that seems to me significant. You seem to think that experience is some commodity – that can be sought! One can respond only to certain circumstances; just what the barriers are, and where the boundaries cross can never be completely known. And the surest way to frustrate the possibility of any free realization is, it seems to me, to wilfully direct it. I can't help it if you think me aimless and irresponsible. But try and see if you get such logical answers always from Nature as you seem to think you will! My 'alert blindness' was a stupid ambiguity to use in any definition – but it seems to me you go in for just about as much 'blind alertness' with some of your expectations.

If you knew how little of a metaphysician I am in the scholastic sense of the term, you would scarcely attribute such a conscious method to my poems (with regard to that element) as you do. I am an utter ignoramus in that whole subject, have never read Kant, Descartes or other doctors. It's all an accident so far as my style goes. It happens that the first poem I ever wrote was too dense to be understood, and I now find that I can trust most critics to tell me that all my subsequent efforts have been equally futile. Having heard that one writes in a metaphysical vein the usual critic will immediately close his eyes or stare with utter complacency at the page – assuming that black is black no more and that the poet means anything but what he says. It's as plain as day that I'm talking about war and aeroplanes in the passage from 'F & H' ('corymbulous formations of mechanics,' etc.) quoted by Wilson in *The New Republic*, yet by isolating these lines from the context and combining them suddenly with lines from a totally different poem he has the chance (and uses it) to make me sound like a perfect ninny. If I'd said that they were Fokker planes then maybe the critic would have had to notice the vitality of the metaphor and its pertinence. All this ranting seems somehow necessary. . . . If I am metaphysical I'm content to continue so. Since I have been 'located' in this category by a number of people, I may as well go on alluding to certain (what are also called) metaphysical passages in Donne, Blake, Vaughan, etc., as being of particular appeal to me on a basis of common characteristics with what I like to do in my own poems, however little scientific knowledge of the subject I may have. [. . .]

To Mrs T. W. Simpson – 4 July 1927

Dear Aunt Sally: Sunshine and a certain amount of heat seem to stimulate me to writing, that is, judging by the intensive work I did on the Island with you last summer, and by the returned activity I've been having lately. We haven't had any particularly hot weather, but it's been warm enough to sweat a little, and that seems to be good for me. As a little evidence of my activities I'm enclosing a new section of *The Bridge* called 'The River.' It comes between 'Van Winkle' which I sent you in the last letter and the Indian 'Dance' which you are familiar with.

I'm trying in this part of the poem to chart the pioneer experience of our forefathers – and to tell the story backwards, as it were, on the 'backs' of hobos. These hobos are simply 'psychological ponies' to carry the reader across the country and back to the Mississippi, which you will notice is described as a great River of Time. I also unlatch the door to the pure Indian world which opens out in 'The Dance' section, so the reader is gradually led back in time to the pure savage world, while existing at the same time in the present. It has been a very complicated thing to do, and I think I have worked harder and longer on this section of *The Bridge* than any other.

You'll find your name in it. I kind of wanted you in this section of the book, and if you don't have any objections, you'll stay in the book. For you are my idea of the salt of all pioneers, and our little talks about New Orleans, etc., led me to think of you with the smile of Louisiana. [. . .]

To Allen Tate – 13 July 1930

Dear Allen: Your last good letter and the admirable review of *The Bridge* in *The Hound & Horn* deserved an earlier response, but time has somehow just been drifting by without my being very conscious of it. For one thing, I have been intending to get hold of a copy of *The Hound & Horn* and give your review a better reading, before replying, than I could achieve at the tables in Brentano's when I was in town about two weeks ago. I still haven't a copy and consequently may wrong you in making any comments whatever. But as I don't want to delay longer I hope you'll pardon any discrepancies.

The fact that you posit *The Bridge* at the end of a tradition of romanticism may prove to have been an accurate prophecy, but I don't yet feel that such a statement can be taken as a foregone conclusion. A great deal of romanticism may persist – of the sort to deserve serious consideration, I mean.

But granting your accuracy – I shall be humbly grateful if *The Bridge* can fulfil simply the metaphorical inferences of its title. . . . You will admit our age (at least our predicament) to be one of transition. If *The Bridge*, embodying as many anomalies as you find in it, yet contains as much authentic poetry here and there as even Winters grants, – then perhaps it can serve as at least the function of a link connecting certain chains of the past to certain chains and tendencies of the future. In other words, a diagram or 'process' in the sense that Genevieve Taggard refers to all my work in estimating Kunitz's achievement in the enclosed review. This gives it no more interest than as a point of chronological reference, but 'nothing ventured, nothing gained' – and I can't help thinking that my mistakes may warn others who may later be tempted to an interest in similar subject matter.

Personally I think that Taggard is a little too peremptory in dispensing with Kunitz's 'predecessors.' We're all unconscious evolutionists, I suppose, but she apparently belongs to the more rabid ranks. I can't help wishing I had read more of Kunitz before seeing her review. He is evidently an excellent poet. I should like to have approached him, not as one bowing before Confucius, nor as one buying a new nostrum for lame joints. Taggard, like Winters, isn't looking for poetry any more. Like Munson, they are both in pursuit of some cure-all. Poetry as poetry (and I don't mean merely decorative verse) isn't worth a second reading any more. Therefore – away with Kubla Khan, out with Marlowe, and to hell with Keats! It's a pity, I think. So many true things have a way of coming out all the better without the strain to sum up the universe in one impressive little pellet. I admit that I don't answer the requirements. My vision of poetry *is* too personal to 'answer the call.' And if I ever write any more verse it will probably be at least as personal as the idiom of *White Buildings* whether anyone cares to look at it or not.

This personal note is doubtless responsible for what you term as sentimentality in my attitude toward Whitman. It's true that my rhapsodic address to him in *The Bridge* exceeds any exact evaluation of the man. I realized that in the midst of the composition. But since you and I hold such divergent prejudices regarding the value of the materials and events that W. responded to, and especially as you, like so many others, never seem to have read his *Democratic Vistas* and other of his statements sharply decrying the materialism, industrialism, etc., of which you name him the guilty and hysterical spokesman, there isn't much use in my tabulating the qualified, yet persistent reasons I have for my admiration of him, and my allegiance to the positive and universal tendencies implicit in nearly all his best work. You've heard me roar at too many of his lines to doubt that I can spot his worst, I'm sure. [. . .]

To Solomon Grunberg – 20 March 1932

[. . .] Peggy and I are still very happy together here. [. . .] We've known each other for nearly 12 years, intimately – but never dreamed, of course, of our present happy relationship. How permanent that will be is far from settled; but we have learned to enjoy the present moment without too much romanticizing – which I think is wisdom.

Wish you could see – and smell – all the delicious flowers that surround our house: calla lilies, freesia, roses, calendulas, white iris, violets, cannas, a dozen colors of geraniums, pansies, feverfew, candy tuft, morning glories, etc. The days are getting warmer and all the deciduous trees are back again in fresh leaf. My fellowship is about terminated, but I expect to stay on here for several months longer if the income from my father's estate seems to warrant. Am even thinking of making my permanent home here. Mexico gets into your veins. Beautiful people, manners, scenery, speech and climate. [. . .]

A way, way back you asked me a question about what I thought of *Moby Dick*. It has passages, I admit, of seeming innuendo that seem to block the action. But on third or fourth reading I've found that some of those very passages are much to be valued in themselves – minor and subsidiary forms that augment the final climacteric quite a bit. No work as tremendous and tragic as *Moby Dick* can be expected to build up its ultimate tension and impact without manipulating our time sense to a great extent. Even the suspense of the usual mystery story utilizes that device. In *Moby Dick* the whale is a metaphysical image of the Universe, and every detail of his habits and anatomy has its importance in swelling his proportions to the cosmic rôle he plays. You may find other objections to the book in mind, but I've assumed the above to be among them, at least, as I among others that I know, found the same fault at first. [. . .]

To Caresse Crosby – 31 March 1932

[. . .] My Guggenheim Fellowship terminates today. But I am remaining a while longer in Mexico on the modest income afforded me from my father's estate, since his death last July. At that time I came North for two months, but was very glad to get back here again as soon as possible. Mexico with its volcanoes, endless ranges, countless flowers, dances, villages, lovely brown-skinned Indians with simple courtesies, and constant sunlight – it enthralls me more than any other spot I've ever known. It *is* and isn't an easy place to live. Altogether more strange to us than even the orient. . . . But it would take volumes to even hint at all I have seen and felt. Have rung bells and beaten pre-Conquistadorial drums in firelit circles at ancient ceremonies, while rockets went zooming up into the dawn over Tepoztlan; have picked up obsid-ian arrows and terra-cotta idols from the furrows of corn-fields in far valleys; bathed with creatures more beautiful than the inhabi-tants of Bali in mountain streams and been in the friendliest jails that ever man got thrown in. There is never an end to dancing, singing, rockets and the rather lurking and suave dangers that gives the same edge to life here that the mountains give to the horizon. Harry would have adored it – past expression – and I am sure you would. I should like to stay indefinitely. [. . .]

To Mrs T. W. Simpson – 26 April 1932
[*Havana, Cuba; postcard*]

Off here for a few hours on my way north. Will write you soon. Am going back to Cleveland to help in the business crisis. Permanent address – Box 604, Chagrin Falls, Ohio.